D1638986

The Wigbox:
New & Selected Poems

This book is to be returned on or before
the last date stamped below.

Acknowledgements
Some of the poems have appeared in *Smiths Knoll* and in
The British Council Anthology of New Poetry, nos. 6 and 8.

Previous publications:
A Woman's Work (Brazen Voices 1984)
Homewards (Giant Steps 1987)
Kill the Black Parrot (Littlewood Arc 1993)
James Naylor (Sessions 1993)
The Underhill Experience (Smith/Doorstop 1995)
The Children's Game (Smith/Doorstop 1998)

The Wigbox:
New & Selected Poems

Dorothy Nimmo

Smith/Doorstop Books

Published 2000 by
Smith/Doorstop Books
The Poetry Business
The Studio
Byram Arcade
Westgate
Huddersfield HD1 1ND

ISBN 1-902382-24-2

British Library Cataloguing-in-Publication Data. A catalogue
record for this book is available from the British Library.

Typeset at The Poetry Business
Printed by Peepal Tree, Leeds

Smith/Doorstop are represented by Signature Books, 2 Little Peter
Street, Manchester M15 4PS, and distributed by Littlehampton
Book Services Ltd, tel. 01903 828800

The Poetry Business gratefully acknowledges the help of Kirklees
Metropolitan Council and Yorkshire Arts.

The cover design is a tile picture by Maggie Berkowitz
Cover photograph by Fred James

CONTENTS

from The Children's Game (1998)

New Poems

The Dorset Conversion

Even second-hand, cannibalised,
even in a junkyard, even
a completely different model,
the new one with the sliding door
and the passage between the front seats.

Even though the children would be jammed
in the back behind the table
while I fried eggs rain fizzing in the hot fat
and everything I needed was in one of the lockers
and somebody was sitting on it.
Even though the starter was
intermittently faulty. Even though it stranded us
in Normandy, in Ilkley, on the Cap d'Agde.
Even though I'd scraped the paint off
on the gatepost in Cambridge. Even though
you sold it when the boy was ten,
We don't keep anything longer than ten years.

Or perhaps because.
Because I've forgotten you
and the children have grown up
and things have changed, a Volkswagen Traveller
is sort-of heartbreaking.

Good Gifts

He gives her a black lace bra:
her heart swells. She fills the C-cup.

He gives her a bottle of champagne
costing £24.50. He has got a bargain.

He gives her a basket of strawberries.
Open wide! he says, gently. She opens.

He gives her a smooth round bloodstone
to wear round her neck. So cold.

He gives her a little house. All day long
she cleans his fingerprints from the paintwork.

He gives her five gold rings, one in her ear,
one in her nose, one in her nipple,

one in her navel, one in her finger. He takes
a fine gold wire and threads it between

ear, nose, nipple, navel and finger.
He twitches the end. She dances.

Conjunctions

Because I can't remember the word
the door must stay shut. Because I have lost the key
the car won't start. Because I have forgotten
the number I can't ring you. Because
I wasted my time time has run out.

Although I wrote the word down I lost
the piece of paper. Although I taped the key
under the dashboard it has fallen off. Although
I think it could have been you who phoned me
I couldn't get there in time.

Between the planning and the installation
there have been changes. Between here
and my destination is a hundred miles.
Between us we seem to have made a disaster.
The spaces between the stars are great black holes.

Ill-Wishing Him

I'm going to have to leave you, he said,
very politely. *Sorry.*

I stood up to riddle the Aga,
to draw the red curtains I'd bought
ready-made, marked down, to put out
the cat and I said, *Oh really? When
were you thinking of going?*

As if I might offer to take him
to the station. As if I didn't want
to make him angry in case he left me.

I wish I'd said, Get out. Now.
In his pyjamas. In the rain.
Scrabbling in the gravel for his toothbrush.
Begging for a change of underpants.

I wish he'd had to rent a room
in Peterborough, to take his washing
to the launderette, watch his shirts turn pink.
I wish he'd lived on pork-pie and pizza
and it had made him sick.

I wish he'd gone senile and forgotten
who he was and what he'd done
and every day I could remind him. I wish
he'd died and left my name
as next of kin. They'd ring me
and I'd say, *Never heard of him.*

Again

It's nowhere near morning. Something
out in the garden. That tomcat? Halfway
down the stairs I trip on the carpet,
clutch the bannister, go down
the rest of the way gingerly.

A truck grinds along the bypass.
The kitchen flags are icy. And there
in the amber light from the carpark
a long time ago he is crushing
my little plants with his great feet,
face against the glass, miming
turning the key, mouthing
Let me in!

I turn, the washing on the rack
brushing my face with the smell
of cut-price detergent, the Rayburn
comforting my left flank, and go
upstairs. Get into bed. Hear him
shifting the furniture back the way it was.

Last Thing At Night

Great Aunt Emma, fearing an intruder,
would kneel down and push her stick
under the bed. Night after night, year after year
there was nothing. But one night
Great Aunt Emma, squat in her winceyette,
pushing her stick under the bed
hit something soft, unyielding. *Come out,*
Friend, she said, *I've been looking for thee*
for fifty years.

Last thing at night I carry the cat upstairs
and open the window. Wind in the birches.
Yellow light from the carpark. I hold the cat
against my chest like a furry breastplate.
I shout: *Is anyone out there?*

He says, *Nobody here but us chickens.*

I say, *Come on up then,*
chicken.

Nanny

Late August, the time when one begins to think
about summer being over and school beginning,
the trunks laid out on the landing and sewing on
the name tapes. I have had questionnaires addressed

to me by name: tick the box that is nearest
to your experience. If none write none.
The apples have not been pruned for ages
and you can't tell any longer where the graves are.

They sent me the cup and saucer with the blue flowers
I gave her one Christmas, with love, I thought.
It gave me quite a turn. My hand trembled and I was like
(would have liked) to have dropped it.

They find me in the conservatory full of dead
geraniums, light striking on all sides. I loved them
well enough, James, Nell, Blossom, but they greet me
as a stranger and politely put me away.

Christmas Poem

This time of year things
are all wrapped up.
It's the end.
It's dark and everything
is wrapped up ready to be delivered.
We are expecting Joy, Grace,
Lucia, Nicholas, Holly, Carol, Gloria,
Claus and Daddy if he can get through

But it's for the children really.
They're swallowing everything, living
in the present, wallpaper striped
scarlet and gold, tinsel and glitter,
the conservatory like the inside of a glass ball
and all the kitchen equipment matching, stainless,
and all hoping for the best. Listen!
It's the thought
that counts.
a one,
a two,
a three and

Now! says Noel, This very morning!
Here's the present! He opens his bag
and the cat scrambles out. Just what they wanted!
But much much too expensive.

My Sainted Aunt

I retraced the journeys pencilled
on National Geographic maps
pinned around the lavatory walls –
Boston, New York, Richmond, Indiana,
Philadelphia, Cape May
and came eventually to the Centre.

Posies of fresh flowers before her picture,
like we had at home, on the hallstand;
that smell of potpourri and her eye,
as always meeting mine with a question.

Everyone was sitting quietly
breathing deeply, humming.
I took my part in the ceremony –
half a jam sandwich for a sponge finger,
sharing spoons for the custard.

She had assumed miraculous powers –
almost everyone was on their feet
and feeling much better.
She was last seen ringed with light
balancing on the breakers
the riptide crinkling the surface.

They referred to her as Holy Mother.
I kept a straight face.
They will stay on at the Centre
and make an appeal for funds.

Once I broke one of the good cups,
the ones with gold edges,
and hid it in the shed.

How could it have got there?

How indeed. I wanted her
to have an unkind thought.
Just one. No, I wouldn't confess
that would have missed the point
and she would have forgiven me.

I plan further journeys.
She must be somewhere
and this is the only map I have.

An Exhibition of Baskets

Invited inside the woven interiors
of egrappori, ukhamba, kisine, angami-naga,
herring cran, panier Perigordian,
imbenge of mala palm, willow and bark bowl,
star-grass pot, trug and string bag
I put on little newspaper shoes,
a hat of plaited reed and cured leather
and creep through doors like eel-traps
towards the inner chamber where the feast
is laid out on the messob.

I curl up inside the Moses basket,
dilly bag at my side, my heart
caught like a fish in a herring swill,
steam-bent hazel boiled and riven.

·

Kevin

is wearing his rubber gloves and a waterproof apron
bent over the sink after the early breakfasts.
The oven door's not shutting again so I kick it
and lean across Kevin to reach the steamer.
'Today' on the radio over the rumble rumble
of the Magimix overloaded with bread dough
and the smell of the second batch of scones
just slightly scorched but they won't complain
as long as we keep down the prices.

Kevin is wearing his cashmere sweater,
I tell him I really like that colour
it goes with his eyes and we laugh and begin
to play clichés. *Soon be Christmas*, he says
and I say, *The nights are drawing in* and he says
It never rains but it pours and I say, *Better
the devil you know* and he says *I don't blame you.*

September 1939

William Watson is out in the garden
burning old copies of Peace News,
petitions, manifestos, resolutions and declarations.

Rosemary Watson turns off the wireless,
checks the blackout and looks out of the landing window
worried about William. They have been praying for months.

William served in the Ambulance Brigade last time
and he remembers. They thought the Lord
wouldn't let it happen again. Now it has happened

and the Lord is still Himself and lets things happen
as is His way, taking no notice of William who struggles
painfully with another box of pamphlets.

Burning, burning! The carton falls on his foot. He curses it
and God and the rain which is putting the fire out.
His face is all twisted and dirty. Rosemary Watson

comes down the garden and takes him by the arm
to lead him back, she hopes, eventually, to a place of safety.

Leavins

The signs: clear weather, swallows back,
oak out before the ash.
Looks like a flocking year, we say
and next thing sure enough there they are
over on the other side with their crates and rucksacks.

So we lay on beer and have us a spread,
Sarah makes Flocking Cake, like a Simnel
but without the marzipan. And there's ham.
Whoo-hoo! Happy flocktime! Here we go again.

It starts quite quiet, a sort of murmur.
Or a groan. Then twittering, like a whole tree of starlings
and louder and louder until it's screaming
and then it's trumpets. And a big drum,
ba-boom, ba-boom across the water.

They go up and down, up and down.
When it gets light, you see them
lying about like washing.

After a while, could be a week
or more, the sound changes.
There's a flute, thin and reedy, and something
that sounds like a zither. And it's so sad.

Next morning the hillside's bare and later
the whole village goes over for the leavins.
We pick it off the gorse and the blackberries
and bring it back in bin-liners.
Erin and Sarah set to, spinning it up,
Jean weaves the cloth, a sort of glittery grey,
Isabel sews the coat.

And the Dreamer puts it on.
She sings us over and we leave it there
and then it's gone.

How long before they come back?
As long as it takes
for their old dreams
to wear thin.

Holed Up

You can't get out so make the best of it.
Find the chess-set and the jigsaws.
Check the camping-stove. Put on extra woollies.

It's going to be a long haul; you'll be sorry
if you finish everything up the first day.
Ration the food. Make a timetable.

There's no point struggling to the shop
it will have sold out except for birdseed
paper towels and detergent.

Make use of what's available. One winter
I painted the kitchen four different colours
to use up the old emulsion.

If the electric fizzles out draw lots
which of the chairs to break up.
Think of it as a challenge.

It will remind you of wartime
if you are old enough. If not
I will remind you.

If you hear a helicopter
spread out a counterpane. The blue
will show up nicely.

Nothing more delicious than that last bit
of potato stuck to the pan. The heel
of a loaf, toasted, between us.

Draw the curtains to keep the heat in
and deal me another hand.
Do that jigsaw again.

Beyond Huddersfield

Beneath the open sky
    me

Under a cloud
    the circumstances

Within limits
    possibility (the bounds of)
    reason

Against (a judgement)
    (a decision)
    one's will

Upon a journey (to set out)
    my word
    my own feet
    a time (once)

Between the rock and the hard place
    friends
    these four walls (just)

Inside out
    the whale

Upside down (a world turned)

Outside my experience
    (there is a world)

Beyond words
belief

The Wig Box

You enclose your head in a cardboard box   *headcase*
sealed with masking-tape.
You need your head examined, you must
take it to the clinic for diagnosis.   *case-study*
Wrap the report-file in brown paper
sealed with masking-tape.   *study-pack*

Liberate a rat from your departmental maze,   *pack-rat*
put it in a box secured with masking-tape.
It may have access to a mobile phone.   *ratline*
Someone at the door in the small hours.   *rat-a-tat*
The rat has complained.   *rat-fink*

Under a single arc-light you should give away   *overhead*
nothing except your name if any.
It will hurt you a lot more than it hurts him.   *headman*
Drape yourself in cotton, an overall pattern   *overall*
on a black ground tied round the waist because
it's all over, your overall taped round your knees
so as not to offend spectators.

You are addicted to print. You have read so much   *bookcase*
you can't distinguish what you know   *overbooked*
from things about which you have information.
The publisher has refused your thesis.   *bookstall*
You don't remember the title.

It's more than you can face.   *over-face*
You can't keep your countenance.
You can't keep your feet. Wrapped in straw   *overwinter*
stored in a cool dry cellar waiting for the spring
when the daffs, bless them, flash away
so gloriously yellow, you faintly remember
something about daffodils but not word for word,
more a kind of fluttering because your ears are shot.   *earshot*
You are advised to wear an ear-wig they make   *earwig*
exceptional mothers but you are beyond caring.

Lifeclass

You suggest I start with charcoal. Get used
to working with the whole arm, moving
freely from the shoulder.

You tell me I am making decisions
with every black mark on the thick grey paper.
Notice the relationships.

Map the connections. My paper is covered
with black decisions. *Do you have
a putty rubber? It's not so much a question*

of learning to draw as of learning to see.
I am to think of the model
as an object in space. When you lean over

I can smell the soap in your wrist-hairs.
You say, *Do you mind if I make these marks
on your work?* I say, *Don't touch me.*

Marvellous Boy

Twenty-four inches long,
his toes sucked lemon-drops, the space
between his eyes smooth and golden
as the heart of a lotus, his skin
tight as an aubergine's, smile
bright as young beech leaves, legs
creased like a sumo wrestler's,
he smells of fresh bread. He is
a mouthful of green peas, the first
strawberry, sweet as cream.

I mind him all day long so I know him
by heart and when he runs away
I'll remember exactly how he went.

Roger on Tuesday

The boy and I stomp steadily
from one thing to another: the shop
with the tiny dogs and cows, the one
with the tractors, the market, the newsagent,
the garden, the river, the slide, the swings.

We stop at the same places every time
to see if they are still the same
and they always are. The boundary's
at the other side of the playground but
we don't need to go as far as that.

In good time you'll have learned how it goes,
that slow progress under the arch into the garden,
birds, leaves, snails, stones, a holding light.
You'll know where you are: that place is always
and ever, asks nothing, expects nothing
and is to the greater glory of God.

Roger's Words

He comes with handfuls of grass and says
flowz; he brings me an apple and says
owl. We take it to be crunched
in big yellow teeth and he says *ors*.
The trough fills, I roll up his *leaves*
and he drops *owns* in the water.
And it's hometime but he says *no*.

He offers me his words and I include them,
in today's special edition; they'll be out of date
in a month. I want to make them last, I suck them
like gob-stoppers, tasting the sweetness, taking them out
from time to time to see how they're doing
until there's only a thin transparent splinter to crunch
between my teeth, swallow and say *all gone* ...

Treats for Roger

I'm going to take these home for you,
all tied up in bright ribbons so when
you come over on Tuesday, stumping
up in your green wellies shouting
HI GRANDMA, HI GRANDMA, WHAT YOU DOIN'?
I'll say Open it! Here's a whole lot
new ones you haven't tried yet.
What do you think of scowl?
How about enormous, already?
Do you fancy horrible? Muggins?
Get your tongue round succulent.
You can play with them all day
improvisation, fortissimo, struggle.

A Photo of Roger

He drapes himself over his mother, says. No.
We just want him to behave himself,
to be a good boy. Our mouths are set,
we bribe, coax, threaten but he can't behave himself,
he has too much sense of himself
that he mustn't betray if it's to come to good.

In this space full of images of people
dressed up as people he takes himself away,
at the end of his tether: *'What I am going to do now*
I'm going down field, with my tractor.
I'm going down to bring cows in,
That's what I'm going to do.'

His self (his true self, full of pain and fear,
sensitive and self-centred as it must be)
is no good to us; he moves away into his own space,
abandons us and our own selves are full of pain and fear,
sensitive and self-centred as they must be.

Small

That morning
just before dawn
(which was late, midwinter
her second year) we saw
her eyes (her eyes
the clear blue of sky
just before dawn)
were not right.

Saying it
because that's how
you come to bear it.
Saying the words:
That Morning.
Saying: not right.
Fourteen months old
and her name was
Sarah.

Head full of nursery rhymes and
cradle songs, small small
feathers a little down and down
she goes, over she goes, this precious
for the third time she goes
down. Small small.

Hannah's Birthday. August 1997

Hi, Hannah!
How do you do?
Happy Birthday! You are
wholly welcome, dear
heart. I wish you
hardihood, good
health, a rich
harvest. Here's a bunch of
heartsease, heather, heliotrope,
honeysuckle, hyacinth,
hyssop, hellebore and self-
heal.
Hark! Hautboy, harp,
harpsichord
hail you while hawks,
hummingbirds, herons
hover over
head. I plant a
hedge of hawthorn,
hazelnut and holly against
hurts, guard your
houseplace from
harm with
hounds, horses
hedgehogs, hares and
hamsters. I wrap you in
homespun and feed you
honey.

Here you are,
Hannah. Give me a
hug. Sing
Hallelujah!

Hush now.

Anopthalmia

The skull.
The sockets where the eyes will be.

But here you will notice
(when your attention is drawn to it
with a shadow-pointer
on the brilliant screen),
here you will notice
that space is blank.

It's not the worst thing
that can happen. Dead is worse
and she is alive inside there, look
at her little hands.

In the womb
we are all blind
as moles;
not to have eyes is something
she must learn to live with
if she is to live at all.

She will be only as
blind as a mole,
digging herself out
her hands
pale as roots.

Can't close my eyes some nights,
prop my lids with matchsticks
not to miss anything
and catch it in the corner of my eye
slipping behind the skirting.

Lambing, if it does wrong
It's almost always better
to get cut your losses.
Can't win them all,
this one will never do. We put
the dead ones in the corner
of the yard and any sheep
that don't make it. That's right.
The huntsman picks them up.

I wouldn't leave her
in the yard.

I have eyes only for her.

Eyes of lapis
of cornelian set
in alabaster fringed
with gold strands.
Exquisite. Or painted
with a very fine brush,
or applique, silk scraps,
blue beads glued
or feather-stitched
with a fine thread. It can be done

But she will hear
the buds open, worms
working their way
to the surface,
bubbles breaking,
thunder behind the hills.

When one door shuts
another opens.

The door slams
her back chills,
she turns and feels her way
across the room
scrambles upon the sill,
her sunbonnet
shadowing her face,
round tinted glasses
hooked behind perfect ears.

I don't feel myself at all
I inch my fingers up and down my body
feel only strange and spend hours
looking at my hand my right hand
the veins prominent,
the knuckles beginning to thicken.

The eye doesn't see the heart
doesn't grieve Such a happy child,
always cheerful, pink bonnet
pulled low over tinted glasses.
Nothing bothers her.

An extremely rare condition
so much so it must be regarded
as statistically insignificant.

Insignificant, notwithstanding
her small hands are pink as icing-sugar.

If insecticide had been a factor the condition
could be expected to be much more common.
Pregnancy should routinely be avoided
in the lambing season.

No-one can be protected from risk.
There is a far greater chance
of being run over by a bus.
Pain is caused by unrealistic expectations.

Two arms, two legs, two ears, ten toes,
eight fingers, two thumbs. Two eyes.
Minimum.

Alice Is Not Herself

blown backward by a wind that changes and
she's stuck like that just as her Granny said,
half her head shaved, the long black top-knot plaited
with strips torn from old sheets, her face
white as a sheet, her eyelids green, with not
so much as a backwards glance (would she
have seen him, did she try to run?) blown out.

Her friends laid wreaths in the culvert under
the rank green murderous elder by
the sluggish Severn. Months later flower
faces blacken under the shiny ever-
lasting wrap, the long white satin ribbons.

Winter floods leave standing water.
Hawthorn slants windward, white ribbons
knotted in long black flowing branches.

Third Daughter

Elsie and Rosie go up the garden
to make secret houses in the bracken.
I climb the gate to watch them go.
What do they do all day?
Wear out their shoes.

Under the netting hot thin-skinned currants
tense with seeds. *Rub in with the fingertips*
says Rosie, *Roll out on a floured board.*
When ready cut into bite-size pieces
using a sharp knife. Red juice runs.

Elsie's name is Secret; she will keep it
as she keeps all her secrets.
She makes my wedding dress, her mouth
pinned up. It is so tight I wonder
how I am meant to run.

Sister

What I feel for you is not love exactly
but I would like to hear from you again,

your voice hooting from a distance
like those trains across the Far Field

in that hard place where we found ourselves,
where we passed in the corridors without speaking

and were not allowed to sit together. The conversation
at meals prepared us for what we must expect.

We learned to be cold and stiff. To observe distance.
Outside in the playground the swing hung in its chains,

the flannels froze overnight as we slept
in our separate houses under those strict blankets.

You said I could go home if I was not happy
which was not true. What I felt was not love

exactly. I thought you might take my hand
and lead me down Driffield Terrace to the station.

I know now you could not have learned
that kind of behaviour in that kind of place.

We have changed our names. Only by chance
would we come together now on any list, in any order.

Pretend Games

You have to be the Princess.
Your mother has tied you to a tree.
The dragon comes down the hill
breathing fire. I'll be the dragon.
You are afraid. HAAAH! HAHA!
Hot hot hot. Go on, struggle.

Now I'm the Prince and you
can go on being the Princess. Snick snack!
The dragon's head is rolling down the hill
like a pace-egg and his blood
runs cold and turns to water.

Alice ran ahead of me out of the dawn wood
the tops of the bracken shook.
I ran after her calling and calling her name
but I couldn't catch up.

We run after our big sisters
calling their names but they don't stop.
They just change their names.

       *   *   *

She says: *You must be Anna.*

We met as strangers, as friends of a friend.
but recognised each other
by a strangeness in the dress,
an intentional simplicity
tailored against the movement of the body,
a sense of something concealed.

Who else could you be?

I had been Talitha for some time,
a dead girl dancing from my grave
perfectly preserved as if
I had only fallen asleep.
Weaving patterns with the loose end of my shroud
What had got into me?

She called my name
over the bare bones of her landscape.
Let me hear from you.
You must be Anna.

      *   *   *

I came up out of my dark place,
drove up a valley where clear water
scoured the stones. The road twisted cruelly
over the crest of a hill. The distance
opened out. I drove myself down
towards her house.

The door opened the wrong way.

She said, Help yourself.

I said, *Take me apart,*
I've lost my place.

A cold kitchen.
Outside we see darkness.
Snow nudges the window.

I want you
against the light. Eyes shut,
palms half an inch from mine
and we will begin to move
together. I don't need to touch you.

Hand against the wall now.
Increase the pressure. Release
and feel your arm drift
upwards. You are light.
Anna is a child of light. Say that. Again.
What do you say?

Thank you.

Feel free.
When I say Go
I want to see you get away.

Do you mean that?

There was a very small crack in the wall
and I found a nailfile in my sock.
So I loosened stone after stone
collecting the mortar in small plastic bags
which I emptied out behind the midden.

I was getting smaller and smaller
until after some time I could wriggle through
and pick my way across the yard
keeping well in under the wall
out of sight of the kitchen window
and squeeze under the gate.

I went up the field track on all fours
my petticoats torn off by the brambles
my hands bleeding.

Who do you think you are?

Sestina

When we were young there was this game
we'd play, where the garden
ran wild to the river. Small fish
made rings in the shadow-water, light
fractured the summertime,
clocks clicked the house towards dark.

We would sleep under our dark
duvets, tired by relentless games,
growing taller, until it was time
for us to leave the garden,
the trees, the roses, the underwater light
glinting on shoals of little fish.

Have you gone off to fish?
Do you still get up early in the dark,
creep barefoot in the thin light
while shadows strengthen? What game
are you playing now? Outside the garden
casting your line time after time after time?

Have you caught anything all this time?
Is there, after all this trouble, even one fish?
A tiny one? For you to carry up the garden
grinning, for me to fillet? It's too dark
now to finish this last game.
I tap the cards together, turn off the light.

But this evening, in the thin clear light,
you turn up again. For a long time,
years, I've played this esoteric game
with the cards and the counters like fish,
waiting for you to come in from those dark
hidey-holes you used to make in the garden.

You are outside in the garden,
now – I catch the sharp whiff of ladslove the light
breeze carries over the lawn. It's quite dark.
I knew there would come a time
when you'd have caught every last fish
and there'd be no point going on with the game.

My old love, it's time to give up the game.
I will walk down the dark garden,
hear the fish jump, see the light fade.

from *Homewards (1987)*

Homewards

Sheltered from the world's winds, there
under that small tump, bristle-backed,
is the real right place, the epicentre.

Lighthouse to church-spire, standing-stone to hill-crest,
beacon to beacon along the ley-lines
a sacred webbing stretches across country.

Cat's cradle. Gold threads on her steel needles.
Hear her calling from the secret garden
even from this other summit across the valley

demanding only the correct behaviour,
the necessary lie, the polite evasion –
a small gesture will be sufficient.

How hard it is, going so far. What tension
walking a different path in another direction.

Maternity Benefit

Mother has made you a house to live in
and she'll make sure you live in it.
Mother has made you a bed to lie on,
she'll cut bits off you if they don't fit.

Mother has made you a nice warm coat
she's knitted it up from her own long hair
you must always wear it inside-out
so nobody else will know it's there.

Mother has made you a lovely dinner
of home-made bread and nourishing stew,
Mother has taken a lot of trouble.
So eat her up. She's good for you.

When you go into the world, my darling,
however high, however far
when you look in the mirror every morning
think, Mother made you what you are.

As the tree is bent why so it grows
and by the fruit you know the tree.
Oh what I have made of you, goodness knows
but God forgive what you've made of me.

The Boys and Girls are Going Out to Play

The boys make guns with sticks and blaze away,
imaginary birds flop from the sky.

The girls make houses out of bales of hay,
their skipping games are based on courtship rhymes.

The boys are battering brambles on their way
and slashing trees that hang across the ride.

The girls are ponies all the summer's day
constructing jumps from stakes and garden twine.

The boys are doing wheelies on their bikes
they twist each other's arms behind their backs.

The girls read True Life stories, pick their spots,
iron their blouses, fight their mums and cry.

The boys have big bikes now. Their helmets hide
their private faces. They bomb up the lane.

The girls go soft with love all dressed in white.
Their mothers think this is their proudest day.

The boys meet brick walls head on. And they might
pull through. Or not. They go the bravest way.

The girls meet life head on and they survive
to watch their children going out to play.

Whichever way they go they go away.

How They Kept Christmas

*Katherine and Primrose Compton Burnett locked themselves
in their bedroom on the 10th December 1917 and were
found dead on the 27th.*

They were to be away for Christmas,
announced a fortnight's holiday
in West Wickham but went further
and in a different direction.

Katherine and Primrose (Topsy and Baby)
backs to the wall, hugged each other
breast to breast in their innocent nighties
comforting their cold feet,
all their wounds to the front
where the armour's weakest.
They took a long trip for the time of year
and never a happy morning.

And it's all dark now.
And the same bad season.
All travelling in a homeward direction.
The kitchen knife is ready to hand,
the oven is big enough for the cold turkey,
the hooks in the larder bear the weight of the joint
and the giftwrapped jar in the cupboard
sings out so soft and small: Honey. Honey.

There is a prize for guessing
how many sweets in the jar,
for knowing when to say when
to say enough is enough

Snapshots

The boy
squints from the page.
His second birthday. His
blonde hair falls over screwed-up eyes.
He grins.

His mum
snaps his likeness.
Now she will take the rope
and pull him on his new red truck
back home.

At six
on a sand dune
poised to hurtle down. Now
his Dad clicks the shutter and he
is caught.

Older,
by waterfalls,
his smile's more shy but then
the girl who took his picture took him in
her arms.

Bearded,
face shadowed, wrapped
in orange robes, withdrawn
in a far country. And there's no smile
this time.

Whose hand
holds the camera?
The eyes are distant. Who,
where this snap's taken, knows to lead
him home?

Away
out of focus,
fallen out of frame they
can't catch up with him. He's gone
too far.

The light
can't hold him now.
Under the grass it's dark.
There are no pictures here where he
falls down.

So she
turns the pages
of the photo-album
where her boy smiles and squints against
the sun.

Message for a Daughter

Remember the stories, can you have missed the meaning
of all those metamorphoses, quests, reversals,
disguises, enchantments, dragons and dangerous journeys?

You must have noticed how all the rescuers were white
princes riding on white horses? Seventh sons perhaps but
born winners, though sometimes disguised, frog-faced or beastly.

And the children of the book, the king's daughter, the heiress
slept on the glass mountain safe from the black forest,
the black witches, the sharp edges. Until he kissed her.

And the man who cracked her face with a smile would win her.
He who killed the dragon would bear the treasure away.
Who guessed the riddle wouldn't take no for an answer.

Now see how the king's daughter, waking white with virtue
walks tall and proud through the church to the houseplace,
white linen, white roses, white candles and a gold cradle.

So go as the sun goes, wise daughter, go clockwise;
wrong way round the church is another kingdom, the price
of walking alone is a sword-blade slashing the instep.

Go by the book read over and over at bedtime.
Remember the colour-coding will be important.
Here are the instructions. These are the rules of the game.

Coming Out

There is a door. Believe me. Open it.
You are inside of your own volition.
Can you see light under the lintel?
Run your hand along the doorjamb.
What makes you think you are locked in?
You have no reason. I am trying to help you.

If you shut your eyes you may feel better.
There must be a handle of some sort.
Now, when your fingers fumble
over the latch, sneck, knob, spindle,
see it if turns. Perhaps if you pull
sharply you'll find it gives. There is
almost certainly some special trick
you have to learn. Manipulate,
juggle, shift. Do not lose your head.
Trust me. When the door opens
you will see the assembled faces.

And by their expression you can imagine
what you have become.

Dream Play

I know there's something I must do today.
It's half an hour before curtain rise,
what is my part in this and what's the play?
There is a smell of greasepaint, dust and size.

It's half an hour before curtain rise,
this is the dressing-room I know is mine.
There is a smell of greasepaint, dust and size.
For God's sake tell me, what's the opening line?

This is the dressing room I know is mine,
when they begin I'll recognise my cue.
For God's sake tell me, what's the opening line?
Who am I? What am I supposed to do?

When they begin I'll recognise my cue.
You're on! they whisper and I face the light.
Who am I? What am I supposed to do?
Forgive me, mother. Have I got that right?

You're on! they whisper and I face the light
and say the line that they expect from me:
Forgive me, mother. Have I got that right?
Was it the daughter that I had to be?

I say the line that they expect from me.
My voice is strangled. I'm awake. I shout
*I know there's something I must do today
and I can't do it. You must write me out.*

My voice is strangled. I'm awake. I shout
I know there's something I must do today
and I can't do it. You must write me out.
It's not my part and this is not my play.

from Kill The Black Parrot *(1993)*

March 15th

Going North, a tyre bursts. The car
skids out of control leaps
the central reservation. But I don't intend
to drive up the motorway.

Letters drop innocently through the slot.
Not a final demand, not some obligation
I have overlooked. That small package
does not contain an incendiary device.

On my way to the shops I do not walk
heedlessly into the path of a bus.
The neighbour's dog does not snap at me,
it does not have rabies.

The knife I use for the tomato is not
particularly sharp and does not slip.
The lightly-boiled egg is not
infected with salmonella.

Walking the river path I do not attract
the attention of the tall youths who
push one another, swear, stagger away
not leaving me stunned and bleeding.

At supper I do not choke on a fishbone.
My banana-skin does not fall to the floor.
I do not slip on it. I do not break my hip.

I am not so unwise as to take the electric fire
into the bathroom and balance it
on the edge of the bath.

Lying in the warm soapy water I do not
slit my wrists. I take only one sleeping pill.

Without

In the corner by the toilets
where you go up to the multistorey,
she's hunched up with her head on her knees
and her plastic bag beside her.

He crouches down, his blue trousers
tight over his kneecaps, his keys
hanging from thick fingers.
Are you all right, mother?
She is not his mother.

It's amazing, she used to say,
when they were small and want,
want, want, you know, the way they go?
Want an ice-cream, want a plastic dinosaur,
want a new t-shirt, want a packet of crisps,
want a comic and she couldn't afford
to buy them everything they wanted though
she'd have given them the whole world on a plate
if she could but she used to say,
It's amazing what you can do without.

And it is, amazing.

This Gate Must Be Kept Shut at All Times

Inside
leaves turn golden, turn red, crisp
and fall.

At all times
children flower, pale and fragile,
trundling their tricycles over the bruised grass.

Outside,
on benches, old men smoke, drink cider, piss
in the corners.

At all times
gulls mew, bark, jeer from the rooftops.
At dusk bells ring down changes.

Outside
drunken boys chase one another cursing.

At all times
this gate must be kept shut.

With difficulty, a baulk
jams the two sides together,
a cane wedged through rusty hoops
to stop it blowing open.

At all times
Inside, a wild unsleeping light
on brickwork, pediment and glazing turns
the dying trees to stone.

Doris' Daughter

         is not quite all there but
she runs through the market in a tearing hurry
to get there, full of terrible rage, pushing her baby
blindly over the road in the teeth of the world,
a pink bundle with a small dark face who eyes
the world, already apprehensive, knowing
it will be years before she can run.

         Doris' daughter
yells abuse at the whole world which is out
to get her, she scoops up the baby, holds it close
to her chest as she streaks through the city,
scatheless, as one can pass one's finger through
a candle-flame and not feel pain. But she can't run
fast enough for the baby whose pink stretch-suit
is scorched, whose hair is frizzled, whose cry is frantic.

The Tangles of Neaera's Hair

Neaera
in her flaming hair
clasps salamanders,
triple-toed, only
strong spirits face them out

combs down pale shoulders
amber waterfalls or
on an ebbing tide
emptying the rock-pool bronze
tendrils wavering
set with pearls

pins her love-locks high
cloud-cover parting
a blue streak up there
beyond the cirrus
sickle swifts
continually fly

plaits her hair with serpents
weaves in those dreadlocks all
their lost entangled faces

(keep your eyes closed
climbing up
your fingers crossed)

wild girl her hair
a mess of cirrus
seaweed
flame.

King's Walk, Gloucester

The women can only buy what's on offer
and they must make sure they get their money's worth
because it's the only worth they have.
So they scream at their children strapped
in their pushchairs who have to learn to behave
nicely.

Later the children run screaming on the grass,
fight each other for toy cars, bikes, rubber balls,
as if they knew there was something they were not
being offered. That's quite enough, says Teacher,
but she is wrong. It is nothing like
enough.

But they swallow the rewards they know they have
deserved for behaving so nicely and when
they have eaten everything there's still something
missing, they are still hungry but now (they have
learned to behave) when they scream it sounds like
laughing.

Jumping Off

He never could stand the sight of blood.
I learned to keep my skin unblemished,
my stomach flat, breasts firm, joints supple.
There would be no blood, I promised.
He himself devised this thick dark hair,
these long legs, these slender ankles hung
with silver bells that sing as my feet shift.
I wear his scarlet robe though red is
not my colour. I paint my nipples, dance
myself into the ground.

From the boat moored below the village
we walked through fields of artichokes,
past the grey-green gold-flecked channels
to the Basilica and the Day of Judgement.
Devils probe and prong, flames leap and lick
and we are among the damned. The Lady holds
the child to her breast; one jewelled tear
falls down her splendid cheek. She knows
how it will end.

I let the blood flow. My stomach swells,
my breasts hang veined and heavy, thunder-
thighs spread wide, I grunt. I bear down.
There is a lot of blood.
They shout JUMP, JUMP! but I cannot jump,
for my life I cannot but when fire
scorches your back, when flames lick the stairwell,
when the child must be saved then you will jump
though you break every bone in your body.

The Pottery Lesson

Why do you break your pots as soon as you have made them?

Because they are not right.
Because I don't like them.
Because they don't satisfy me.
They are not the way I want them to be.
They are all crooked.
I am ashamed of them.
I am ashamed of myself.

Those are good answers
but they are not the answer. Why do you break
your pots as soon as you have made them?

Because I have made them.
Because they show too much.
And I don't want to look and
I don't want anyone else to look
because I recognise them
because they are mine.

Those are good answers.
But they are not the answer. Why do you break
your pots as soon as you have made them?

Because when the clay is broken,
soaked in water, wedged on the board
and returned to its original state
it can be used again.

That is a good answer. Still, it is not
the answer. Why do you break your pots
as soon as you have made them?

I can't answer your question.

When you can answer that question
you will no longer be broken.

I Pick Up the Ball

run on the spot bouncing it front of me,
toss it high, catch it with one hand,

spin it on the tips of my fingers,
throw it from one hand to the other,
pass it behind my back,
bounce it between my legs, spin and
sling it underhand to my partner who
drops it.

I laugh, pick up the ball running lightly
in little circles patting it gently.
I toss it in the air, head it twice, steady it
let it roll down my back slowly, slowly.
Arch my back, bounce it off my hip,
to calf, to heel, a sharp kick up and
over to my partner who
drops it.

I pick up the ball keep it in the air
feet going all the time, throw the ball,
catch the ball, turn, twist, spin, catch
it again, make with the wrist, one hand.
two hands AND again, HUP!
Head, nose, hip, shin, knee, elbow, HUP!
and toss it to my partner who
drops it again.

I hold the ball close to my chest.
Couldn't you keep it up?
Couldn't you keep it going?

It was all right on the ground.

But that's not the game!

Were we playing a game?

Rondeau Redouble

There is so little left. The room is bare.
She'll strip his sheets and blankets by and by –
only this morning he was sleeping there.
The light is pouring from a hard white sky.

She'll write to him, perhaps he will reply?
He's better off, she knows, God knows, elsewhere.
She'll be all right she told him cheerfully.
There is so little left. The room is bare.

His smell's still hanging in the chilly air,
his motorcycle boots are propped awry,
helmet abandoned on the basket-chair.
She'll strip his sheets and blankets by and by.

Make a fresh start. Do something useful. Try
to avoid that stunned and slightly foolish stare
the mirror offers her maternal eye.
Only this morning he was sleeping there.

He's left a paperback face downwards where
he gave up reading and she lets it lie.
That's not his footstep coming up the stair.
The light is pouring from a hard white sky.

she stacks up papers, pulls the covers high,
faces the glass now, plucks the odd grey hair,
flicks away cobwebs, dusts off a dead fly,
feels and tries not to feel her own despair.
There is so little left.

from *The Underhill Experience (1995)*

Jo and Mary

He is tall and thin with long clean hands.
His trousers are held up with braces,
he wears clean white shirts,
he is infinitely reassuring, that deep voice,
that small soft beard. He might bring him self
to conceal things *(I saw nothing suspicious,
officer)* but he would not embellish.
He does not understand riddles.
He does not enjoy puns.

Her hair is tied with a blue ribbon,
she wears long skirts, high necks, no make-up,
keeps her eyes lowered and her voice soft.
She does not tell lies either though she might,
in compassion, evade the truth –
It will be all right, you will get better.
If a man should slip on a banana-skin
she would only be concerned
lest he hurt himself.

Such good children, so innocent, so tender.
We will set them up in a decorative niche
lay fresh flowers at their feet. None of us
would be in the least tempted
to paint a moustache on her upper lip
or daub bad words on his waistcoat.

Katherine

I am here because I am old. There is no reason
why I should be here, why I should be alive
but I am here. I am alive.

I kill the hours one after the other This one.
Wring its neck. Eyes glaze. Last spasm of little legs.
Doesn't take long. An hour.

Sometimes I wake up thinking I have died in the night.
You have given me a call. We have a calling.
But there's no call for me.

Sharp pain in the chest. Obstruction in the bowel.
Breathlessness. I would not welcome them but might
be glad to have it over.

I wind my thin hair round my skull, wash my body,
put on clean underwear, skirt, cardigan. I watch
the falling leaves, the squirrels.

Shut my eyes to practise not being able to see.
Am silent, practising not being able to speak.
Sometimes hold my breath.

I am here to find out if there is anything left
when everything is gone. I study my dying.
I am not too old to learn.

Betty

She makes bones from white clay, shaping and smoothing night
after night, underground. The light is dim, the air thick.

Some don't come through the firing. Impurities
in the clay body break under stress.

A single drop of water trapped in the clay
can crack it open. She has survived the firing,

dry-eyed, smoke-cured, her skin like a kippered herring,
fingering the nose-flute, rattling the knucklebones

she beats on a hollow skull with a drumstick, keeps
her spirits up. Outside the leaves fall, golden

under the trees like pools of blood, like tears,
like rain, like leaves.

He knocks. Tries the handle. Waits a minute.
Where is my bone? She has it ready.

Animal Kingdom

Bear's powerful shoulders roll, his paws flatten, his head
weaves, lethal and stupid. Avoid his little blind eye.

Black widow scuttles behind the kitchen sink
on a great many legs. Her kiss is fatal.

Hen harrier laughs harshly and all laugh in chorus.
Head cocked, she tears open the piecrust.

Snake wraps himself round small creatures gently.
His grip tightens and they fall asleep.

Sow wallows, heavy flesh and thick white skin, her pink-
rimmed eyes squinny. She will eat anything. Babies.

Little dog barks, slavers, grins and takes liberties,
sniffs at crotches and abuses cushions.

I keep my mouth shut so they do not see my teeth.
Tiny, malevolent, I could be rat or weasel.

They should hang me up on the fence as a warning.

Karen

She is young, a good child who believes everything
and loves everyone, she feels deeply when she sees
pictures of poor starving people – it's not right, she
says fiercely, it can't be right that we have so much.

Away she goes with her long straight legs, her fine teeth,
her hair like a peaty waterfall, her eyes blue
as blue, as blue as unclouded sky, to the hot
tin-roofed village where she teaches the children.
She has never known such grace in just living, just
being, oh the way they walk with those petrol-tins
on their heads, their pale feet printing the soft red dust.

When a man, a spokesman for the Agency, maybe, or
the young man who is teaching her drums, when he calls
her, *Come, let's make music, have a drink, Coke, OK?*
When he lays his black hand on her white breast she
wouldn't want to hurt his feelings, would she? No,
she loves all men, indeed she does. Is that how it happened?

Or should we imagine a group of boys, *Hey Miss!*
from the other side of the street. They are only
children. *Hey Miss, come see what we got!* But
there are so many of them, white teeth shining and when
she crosses the road they drag her behind a shack
and they show her what they got. Is that what happened?

Back home she gathers round her young men and boys,
her breasts swell her scarlet t-shirt, her nipples are
provocative, she talks dirty. Eyes down they shift
uncomfortably feeling their clothes suddenly tight,
she says words they wouldn't say aloud, makes gestures
they have only made in private and when they blush,
ashamed, and when they squirm and pretend not to be
ashamed she looks at them with those eyes as blue
as blue, as cold as unclouded sky and says
I am not responsible. I am not responsible.

from *The Children's Game (1998)*

The Children's Game

It is the game they play on their days off,
sick days, half-days, early closing days
in the long light evenings
when everything has stopped working.

The boys pretend to be men. They go out.
The girls sing love-love-love and rock the babies.
The boys come back. They pass the babies
round the circle.

When the music stops, whoever is left
holding the baby takes its clothes off.
In the end the baby is naked and
everyone falls down.

In the old days miners
would take a cagebird underground
and as long as it went on singing
they would know they were alive.

Now, in the shopping malls, do you notice babies
in little wheeled cages with plastic covers?
The women push them about and sometimes
they seem to be asleep.

We will finish with dancing.
This is how it goes: hold hands
in a circle. One step forwards,
two steps back. Mark time.

Now the men walk away from the women,
the women walk away from the children
and the children walk away from the old people
and the old people are left shuffling in their cages.

Are they still singing?

Learning the Rules

We never learned the rules. We must have been
away or something when they explained them.
No one had told us how you held your stick,
where you had to stand or what offside meant.
We hadn't got the right equipment
or the right shoes. Ashamed and awkward
we shuffled to the back, were picked last,
dawdled in the outfield, played the fool
and were declared out.

So when there was everything to play for
I thought this was another of those games
I was born to lose. I shrugged you off,
pretended I didn't care, wasn't the type
and never wanted to play in the first place.
I hid in the long grass under the apple trees
until it was too late and everyone had gone home.

Years Later

when I see his writing on an envelope I think,
Oh yes! That was the man I married. I live
so easily without him now that I forget him
for months at a time. Until perhaps some man says
Let me help you.

And I knock his teeth out.

He mops up the blood, bewildered, and I apologise:
I'm so sorry. I just couldn't hear you for the echoes.

Let me help you. Let me do that for you.
You can trust me.

How It Goes

You can tell those people are wearing
period costume by the stilted way they move
but your first dance-dress was like that, pink
taffeta, boned at the waistline.

You had a toaster like that when you were married.
Now it's behind glass. It must be worth something.
Here they have reconstructed the wash-house
and the young woman is wearing Gran's pinny.

That's where you used to stop on the way back from school
to spend your coupons. Look at the little houses.
There are the Uncles in their stiff collars and trilbys.
That's how it was before they built the carpark.

The wedding presents are long ago broken and even
the new chair you bought after the children left home
is shabby. There are things you know you will never do
now, and even more you will never do again.

When you were young you said you would rather die
than live to be old. And yes, perhaps you would rather.

Goodwife

I live in her skin. I look out from her eye-sockets.
I have made her bed, I have slept with her husband.
I knead her bread, I spit on the heel of her iron
and hear it sizzle. I stoke her fire. I slip my hands
into her rubber gloves and plunge them in hot water.
I prune her roses. My feet are heavy in her boots.
I have carried her children.

                    She wraps herself up warm
but I am always cold. She eats but I am always
hungry. She confesses but I am not forgiven.

Hares dance in the furrows, owls haunt the barn, no swifts
nest in the rafters and we have no luck with parsley.
All the yard cats are black, not a white hair on them
and all our children are barren.

Grandmother's Corsets

I wish now I had always worn corsets,
I could pull the laces tight,
I could pull myself together.

My grandmother was a gentlewoman,
she wore mauve and lavender and underneath
pink twill slotted with whalebone.
Her carriage was perfect.

They give me sugar in my tea because I'm powerless.
I have it in mind to think of my grandmother
who said it was always such a comfort
when the time came to loosen her stays.

In Weston-super-Mare we must enjoy ourselves,
it is all we have left to enjoy.
A trip in a coach, the sand, the sea,
the sunshine.

Mrs Anderson showed me where she had caught the sun,
I admired her for that. The fierce sun
had gone all the way down
and left a red mark on her breasts.

It was not necessary to go to Weston I could
have refused though they say there is no alternative.
You have to laugh, don't you? No. There is
always an alternative.

If I were wearing corsets I could remove them.
It would be such a comfort.

A Birthday Present for Roger John

I would like to send you something very small
that you could carry with you always, no trouble at all.

I would like to write something you could learn by heart
without even trying and never forget.

I would give you something you already have
that you would keep for the rest of your life, that isn't mine to give.

I would wish you enough time, enough space,
a strong heart, good spirits, a safe place.

But if you turn out to be left-handed, if you suspect your name
may not be your real name,

if you can hear the cry of bats, if you can dowse
for water, if your dreams belong to somebody else,

if when you stand at the tide's edge looking out to sea
you hear them calling to you, then you must come to me.

Put your hand in mine. I'll say,
It's all right. It's possible. We go this way.

Two Men and a Pig

My name is Joseph Henderson.
My brother here is Matthew Henderson.
Pig's name is McDonald.

I was called after my father.
Matthew was called after our uncle.
Pig was called after the hamburgers.

I weigh twelve-and-a-half stone.
Matthew weighs thirteen odd.
We haven't weighed pig yet.

I am forty-six years old.
Matthew is forty-four.
Pig is ten months.

I am wearing wellies, working trousers,
jacket, cap. Matthew is wearing boots,
waistcoat, no jacket. Pig is naked.

I am standing on the left.
Matthew is standing on the right.
Pig is upside down in the middle.

I am smiling.
Matthew is smiling.
Pig is not smiling.

For All the Saints

They offer him tea and biscuits;
he leaves rings on the french polish and crumbs on the carpet.

They suggest he goes to the night shelter;
he sleeps in the porch and relieves himself in the corner.

They give him a pair of trousers and an old overcoat;
he breaks into the shed. A Stanley knife goes missing.

They lend him five pounds for his ticket to Bristol;
he comes back drunk and breaks the front window.

They say, any time he's in trouble, just to call them;
he rings the bell repeatedly after midnight.

They forgive as they themselves hope to be forgiven;
he uses obscene language and pulls the knife on them.

They call the Social Services and have him sectioned.

Before or After

I like to get there early when the cleaning
has just been done and you can smell polish.
Or when, in the kitchen, cucumber and radish
march all the way down the salmon and the icing
is perfect. Before the shop opens, when pyramids
of apples and oranges still show no sign of blemish.
When the garden's newly raked, the flowers fresh
and nothing has been said that can be heard or misheard.

Or after. When scars of fires and flattened grass
show where the campsite has been abandoned.
When the beds are stripped and the visitors gone.
When the furniture van drives away and the house
echoes like a cathedral. When there's no more traffic.
When everything has gone wrong that's going to go wrong.
All the changes have been rung and weeds begin
to push their way up through the tarmac.

The Spirit of Place

In the end cubicle behind the piano
the wall scored with vertical lines in groups of six.
A seventh diagonally cancels them.

A heavy heartbeat and a faint unmusical wailing.

In the basement someone crouching
between the stored trunks has gouged out the plaster:
a passage through which a thin spirit might escape.

When the battery of the radio is fading, turning it
this way and that, sometimes you catch
distant signals, cries for help. Sometimes only a confused crackle.

A cubby for discarded costumes. Red cloak, flounced skirt,
blankets for Christmas shepherds. Fingermarks
under a skylight stopping short of the catch.

A train breathes heavily and all the wagons clang together
like cracked bells ringing down to silence.

An iron bedstead. A flat pillow. Pulling the knees up,
wrapping the nightgown round the knees, blocking the ears.

Third stall from the door is locked. Peering
under the partition: nothing. Someone crouches
on the lavatory seat, tears paper into small pieces, eats them.

The pipes sob and gurgle. Taps drip.
Wearing the wrong shoes, ignorant of the rules of the game,
scoring the dust with the head of a second-hand racquet.

Screaming like gulls or schoolgirls.

On the fourth panel of the railway bridge the letters SOS.
Arms hitched over the parapet, toes feeling for the strut,
watching the line all the way southwards.

A humming, a vibration, a distant thunder.

Small houses backing the line. Cabbages, runner beans, a row
of washing.
Man in greenhouse, woman moving round kitchen,
children banging in through the front gate.

Home. Home.

My Father's Shadow

At Seascale our shoes were full of sand.
Daddy emptied them out in the front porch
and we went up the stairs like good girls
and pulled the quilts over our heads as
the rocks dragged the dark silk sea back
over the wet ridged sand again
and again and the sea was lovely really.

Mother said, *It's not cold really,*
you'll get used to it, but I was frightened.
Daddy said, *She'll go in when she's ready.*
He found a hollow in the sand
and something sweet in his pocket.

I wouldn't have chosen to grow up
quite this way, to be quite so far out,
to become so used to the cold
that now I can even lie down in the snow
and imagine it's warm. Imagine
I'm in the warm sand
in the shadow of my father.

For Susan and her Mother

My mother's breasts were little purses
nipple-buttoned. Her voice
rang round the house and all the good glasses
up on the top shelf shivered.

I tugged at her skirt. She was about
her Father's business.

When I had daughters I said
I would mind my own business
but as they grew up I watched them
watching me behind closed faces.

Now is the time for our mothers to fall
like sparrows, their feathers numbered.

You carry yours cupped in your hands
to the hilltop and let her go
winging out above the meadows.
What larks, what sadness
what a cold pink sunset.

And down here I pick out bits of glass.
I splash the window-frames with blood,
the doors, the lintels

and those who are wise go past
minding their own business.

Moggy At Grimma's

Fee fi fo fum and look at the plunge in Grimma's Arden.
Watch the slips! They're a bit properly.
The gag won't hurt you, he's a blood boggy.
Flat him. Bently! He won't fight, he's only breaking.
A gnashy noise. Brown, Pincer, brown!
The brass is blush and clamp, The bones are green.

See the clash? Under the breeds?
Goldsplishes and polyglots. Frigs.
All lippery. Mutes under the leaving.
It's all crud at the bottom. Woeful!
Be woeful, brawling, don't want to brumble,
you'll get all brat!

Grimma's mouse smell molishs and purey.
The more's lippery. What's in the hubbub? Names,
sacks of pards, bluedo and pelicans.
When you get colder Grimma will play with you,
snappy fumblies, widdley-tinks, necks and sadders.
You can go worst because you're longest.

The cock kicks. Grimma binds up the cock
with her big clay. She grinds and grinds,
the cock goes knick-knock and the time goes BONG.

Meet your tickys up. Link up your silk.
It's in your very grown hug with the habits on.
How many habits? Gone, who, me. Oh suck
at all those hums! Fetch the weaver,
weep up the hums all sweet and sidey.

Up in the pilchard there are asps
in the blindfold mopples, huzzing in the blowers.

Wipe moreberries under the knotting.
This one's dead. Meet it up, bawling. And a mother!

Look how star you can be from here! Proud arrows
boating over the sills and alleys, folds and goods,
bright out to the freeside across the way.

Roamtime now. Say butterfly to Grimma, wailing.
Grieve her a miss, grieve her a shrug,
sun again moon! She bends by the floor and braves.
She braves and braves as Moggy thrives away.

Cinquaines for Oliver David

Nine weeks:
October to
nearly Christmas. Beloved,
all the days he knew were short
and cold.

We hoped
to exchange gifts –
bread straight from the oven
smelling of yeast, wrapped in a clean
napkin

and fish,
just delivered,
pink, tender: what is this
scorpion? What is this stone, this
hard thing?

We dig
under the wall,
fold back bleached rough grass
hack out a narrow space and make
his bed.

Morning
sunshine. Spring light
is sharp, leaves acid green,
the long-shadowed grass stays wet all
morning.

The Way She Shakes Her Hair Loose

That fine fair hair gathered up,
piled on her head. The way her arms
curve to take out the clasp the way
she shakes it loose.

How seductive
her arms are, that old green sweater
with the sleeves pushed up, the inside
of the elbows peculiarly tender. A tinkle
of silver bangles and her back arches
as she drags the sweater over her head
and shakes her hair loose.

Summer ends.
They plough stubble under, fresh grass
pushing between cut stalks. It rains,
blackberries taste of nothing,
leaves shrivel with the first frost
and beach the marrows. Silver
floods the grassland, the white
specks of seagulls
ride the little waves.

I watch her.
The way she shakes. Her hair.
The way she shakes it loose.

Anna to Margaret

You are the answer to all my riddles,
the master-key to my cipher.
Each rhyme is in relation to your name,
sometimes the sequence of consonants,
sometimes the tune of vowels. The breaks
between stanzas are shaped by your absence.
Each image connects with the next because
you are between them. My found poems
are constructed from your old letters,
your shopping lists, your memoranda.

If I laid out a garden it would include a maze;
in the centre a space only you could fill.
My stage sets would demand you make an entrance.
My songs would be set for your voice.
In my tapestry your initials form the border
entwined with daisies and peacocks.

My pictures would be painted with your colours –
blues, greens, the sheen of feathers.
My abstracts based on the geometry of your body,
parabola of breast, angle of hip, strong
upthrust of hair. The way I apply pigment
corresponds to your gestures, incisive,
erratic, impulsive. The relationship between forms
traces what was once between us.

Your name patterns my landscape, spelled out
in white stones you can see only from the air
or once a year, for a few minutes at dawn
at the time of the solstice. In a dry year
the foundations of our life together
show up in pale markings.

But I read your books as they are published,
haunt your garden, attend your exhibition,
watch your performance, echo your song,
unpick the strands of your embroidery,
fly over your bleak country.
I can find no sign of how it was.
or how it was we became strangers.

Margaret of Anna

When she left there were traces of her
in the upstairs drawers. Hairpins. Pencil stubs.

I made sure I cleaned them away.
The sight of them made me oddly nervous.

I felt she had taken possession and indeed
there was a time when I felt possessed.

There has to be some give and take
between friends. I gave her what I had available:

coffee, banana bread. She refused both;
it was something else she wanted

and that I sometimes wonder if she took.
Because when she left there were things missing.

I've removed all evidence of our relationship,
whatever it may have been, from my records.

I do not read what she writes for fear I might
understand it. I do not open her letters.

I do not remember her. And I would tell her so
but I have lost her address.